Katrina Sculptures

Reflections of the Resilience of
the Mississippi Gulf Coast

Marlin Miller

Dolphin Publishers

This book is dedicated to all the incredible volunteers who have given so much of themselves to help those in need.

"Marlin Miller has shown compassion and dedication to the residents of the Gulf Coast through his work to beautify a storm ravaged area. He took time away from his wife and family to create incredible works of art. His work has been featured on many television stations, radio programs, magazines and news papers around the country, which draws attention to the continually rebuilding effort on the Gulf Coast."

I, Haley Barbour, Governor of the State of Mississippi, hereby proclaim August 29, 2009 as

MARLIN MILLER DAY

And declare Mr. Miller an Honorary Mississippi Citizen.

- Haley Barbour, Governor

Introduction

This all began in 2007 with two trees and branched out from there, growing much bigger than I ever expected or dreamed.

Three years later I've carved a trail of 50 sculptures across South Mississippi and the project continues to shine national attention on the coastline left almost bare by Hurricane Katrina.

The Katrina Sculptures are what remains of trees that were destroyed by the storm carved into turtles, dolphins, egrets and other sea life indigenous to the area. They have become new landmarks and turned the focus from what was lost during the hurricane on August 29, 2005 to what remained.

Miller time

The first sculptures were done when Biloxi Mayor A.J. Holloway hired a chainsaw contractor to carve a group of trees that died from Katrina's saltwater storm surge. The bare trees were in the grass median of Highway 90, also called Beach Boulevard, and were marked for removal.

The summer before Katrina, the people of Biloxi came to help my town of Fort Walton Beach, Florida rebuild after Hurricane Ivan. As an artist and professional woodcarver, I thought carving a couple of the trees before they were chopped down would be a fitting return gift to Biloxi.

After two were carved, I continued to make the three-hour trip from my home to Biloxi most every weekend for two years, carving trees for nearly 40 miles across the beach from Ocean Springs to Waveland and giving them second life.

The story is told

While I returned home to Florida at the end of the weekend, the local media was writing and broadcasting the story of the sculptures and Vincent Creel was posting it on Biloxi's website. Residents saw photographs of the owl and marlins I carved out of the trees so skinny that was all I could shape from their trunks.

I wanted so badly to save one odd-shaped tree that I carved it into a long-necked heron. One writer described it as "Old Mr. Heron walking down the median" and it perfectly described the tree.

When I returned each weekend, more people knew about the carvings from articles in the Sun Herald newspaper and reports on WLOX-TV. Residents who learned I was driving over at my expense and paying for the equipment to do the larger carvings pressed cash and checks into my hands. When I returned their money, I found Christmas cards, jars of jam and other gifts for me at the base of the trees.

Emotion runs deep

There seems to be a lot of crazy emotion surrounding these sculptures. Pass Christian Mayor Chipper McDermott said it's because the oak trees are hundreds of years old and have deep roots, like the people of South Mississippi.

There aren't very many places in this country where you can find people so deeply entrenched in the soil. Biloxi is one of the oldest cities in the country and it's the nature of the people who live there to stay generation after generation, storm after storm.

An elderly woman came up to me at a festival in Biloxi. She had only recently returned to the Coast after being away for a couple of years after Katrina. Her daughter had driven her to see all the sculptures and she was so excited when she came to one of the trees I had carved. She and her sister had played under that tree when they were young girls, probably four generations ago.

The emotion really played out at the Peter Anderson Festival in Ocean Springs. Six or seven times that fall weekend when somebody came to talk to me I was touched so deeply I had to get up and walk away. One time it was a large man who wanted to make sure he was speaking with the guy who had done the sculptures on the highway.

"I just want you to know that you had a really big impact on a lot of people," he said, his voice starting to tremble as tears slid underneath his dark sunglasses. He stopped talking, shook my hand firmly in his big hand, mumbled "thank you" and disappeared into the crowd.

Sculptures branch out

The sculptures touched most of the cities in South Mississippi and many of the events that are so important to the residents, from fishing tournaments to fundraisers for more than two-dozen charities. The mayors made me an honorary citizen and gave me the key to their cities that I now consider my second home.

Word of the Katrina Sculptures started getting out to millions of people across the state and the country when they were featured on Mississippi Roads and NBC Nightly News.

I wanted to bring those already here down to the Coast to increase business for the restaurants, hotels, shops and attractions that were opening again after Katrina. Putting sculptures at the airport and the Mississippi Welcome Center enticed some of those driving the interstate or going straight to the casinos to detour for a look.

One family drives the beach every Sunday. A dealer at one of the casinos has a son who is autistic and for a year or two following Katrina he basically stopped communicating with anyone in any way. This 10-year-old boy started responding to the wood sculptures. It was almost therapy to him. He absolutely loved driving by these sculptures and now a year later his family makes the Highway 90 sculpture run after church.

Engrained in the Coast

The people of South Mississippi have adopted the Katrina Sculptures, decorating them with Santa hats and Mardi Gras beads.

When this year's Hancock Bank calendar came out, Pass Christian Police Chief John Dubuisson, whose wife works at the bank, made sure I got one. "Check out April," he said.

The bank chose landmarks from the whole Southeast, from Florida to Louisiana, and there in April was the sculpture I carved for Col. Lawrence E. Roberts in Pass Christian.

That same month oil started spilling into the Gulf and as dolphins and turtles washed up on the shore, the wooden sculptures were a reminder that these beautiful animals should never be taken for granted.

The book

It started out that I was going to leave a mark on Mississippi with the Katrina sculptures. It quickly flipped around and I was along for the ride on this entire project.

The idea of a book came as a way to honor the people whose stories I heard every weekend as I carved. These aren't professional photos but ones we took as my whole family got involved in the project. Four different covers to let readers choose the one that represents their connection to the trees.

Time and location

If I had done sculptures on the same scale where I live in Fort Walton Beach, Florida or Houston or any other place in the country, I don't think it would have had near the impact. It was the emotion following Hurricane Katrina and the depth of generations the carvings touched.

The Katrina Sculptures never will be duplicated, not because of the artwork, but because of the people who live on the Mississippi Gulf Coast.

CONTENTS

Colonel Roberts Eagle

Robin Roberts was in Gulfport signing her book, "From the Heart: Eight Rules to Live By," when I met her.

The host of Good Morning America started telling the story of South Mississippi and its comeback from Hurricane Katrina the very next day, right after she found her mother, Lucimarian, safe in her home at Pass Christian.

Roberts grew up in Pass Christian and never forgot her roots. Her book is so much about the strength of her parents, Colonel Lawrence E. Roberts, who flew with the Tuskegee Airmen, the first African American pilots to serve in the U.S. military, and Lucimarian, who was chairperson on the Mississippi State School Board and the New Orleans Federal Reserve. They were both very active in the local Boys & Girls Club and the town.

Robin Roberts from "Good Morning America" congratulating Marlin on his sculpture project.

Mary Anne Barkley - Gulfport Galleria of Fine Art, Marlin Miller, Shirley Phipps - Gulf Coast Opera, Elaine Stevens - PR Manager, IP Casino Resort, Rene Miller.

One of the many galas at the Gulfport Galleria of Fine Arts.

Meeting Robin and reading her book gave me the idea to honor Colonel Roberts and his family in a big way. As I carved the other Katrina sculptures in Pass Christian's War Memorial Park, I eyed a huge oak that had died right in the middle of the park. I could see an eagle in it and thought that would be the perfect tribute to an Air Force hero.

I knew Dorothy Roberts McEwen, whose jewelry is on display at the Gulfport Galleria of Fine Art along with my sculptures. She was my go-between with the Roberts family. When she said they were very excited about the prospect of memorializing Colonel Roberts with a carving, I went to work.

Despite what people in other parts of the country believe, Mississippi has winter and the humidity makes it seem even colder. I know what cold is, having grown up on a farm in Iowa, but this was the coldest I've ever been.

Even dressed in heavy shirts and jeans, it was just misery while I carved. The temperature at 4:30 that first morning was 29 or 30 degrees. The north wind chilled it to 19 degrees and blew sawdust in my eyes. I was freezing and had days of work ahead. Although I had never felt that before with any sculpture, I was seriously ready to get in my truck and drive away.

Perhaps the spirit of Colonel Roberts and our shared Air Force history kept me going. I pushed on for another hour and it was like I wasn't alone anymore. Around 6:30 a.m. Pass Christian Police Chief John Dubuisson showed up with coffee, as he did like clockwork the next days. After that the tree just came together.

The large oaks on the coast were embedded with steel, eyehooks, nails, bolts, and even ceramic electrical insulators. Several trees also had rocks and large pieces of concrete. The Katrina sculptures required hundreds of chainsaw chains.

The "green machine" man lift was required for this giant tree. It allowed Marlin to travel high into the sky to get detail on the wing tips.

"What's it going to be?" a man who came into the park later shouted up to me. "It's going to be an eagle," his little boy replied. The child had the vision, and like me could see the eagle before it was carved. Not just an eagle, but what I believe is the World's Largest Wooden Eagle. After much research I couldn't find any larger, so until someone contradicts it, Pass Christian holds the title.

The weekend I finished carving and coating the eagle with marine spar varnish was prom weekend in Pass Christian, and couples in gowns and tuxes came to the park for pictures.

I noticed one mom with a serious camera directing poses so I lowered the lift and asked if she wanted a different angle. I raised the lift until she was able to get a picture of the couple between the soaring eagle wings. Soon I had other mothers lined up, some thinking I was charging people for the photo angle. With sawdust still flying around, I'll bet I brought six or seven moms up in the lift to get prom pictures framed by the eagle wings.

I missed my daughter's prom when I was on the Coast doing carvings, but I got in on the celebration in Pass Christian.

This is some of the equipment that Sculptor Marlin Miller used to carve the Col. Roberts Eagle.

Aerial view of the completed sculpture.

"The very talented Marlin Miller transformed the dead and the ugly, giving it new life in the form of magnificent coastal sea life and native birds. In doing so, he carved joy into the hearts of many. Marlin and his beautiful and talented wife, Rene, are a tremendous team! They are two of the most giving, wonderful, and exciting people I have ever met. I am thankful for their friendship and for their contributions of time and talent to the people of South Mississippi. Katrina thought she had the last word, but she had not heard the mighty saw or seen the Marvelous Marlin Miller at work."

- Mary Anne Barkley

Co-founder, Gulfport Galleria of Fine Arts

Dedication

This one day sticks in my mind more than any other during the more than two years I've spent carving sculptures in South Mississippi.

It was March 28, 2009. Mayor Chipper McDermott put up a tent in War Memorial Park. Subway provided sandwiches. Residents whose homes still stood near the park walked over and joined the others crowded around the Roberts family.

Lucimarian, her three daughters, Dorothy, Sally-Ann and Robin, and grandchildren were there but heavy storms and flooding kept her son, Larry, from attending. The day cleared just in time for the ceremony.

Brigadier General Greg Touhill and several others from Keesler Air Force Base came dressed in their military uniforms to honor Colonel Roberts. Members of the Tuskegee Airmen also were there and the deep voice of Retired Air Force Chief Master Sergeant Christopher Moore filled the park with the National Anthem.

Lucimarian Roberts with her daughters and granddaughter talking about her family's history.

Mayor McDermott dedicating the eagle as the town's residents look on.

Mark Michael, Robin Roberts (with her pen) and Marlin.

Hundreds of people attended the dedication ceremony of the Col. Lawrence E. Roberts eagle.

The day was just so incredible. General Touhill, Mayor McDermott and I spoke about the significance of the tree. When Lucimarian began telling her friends and neighbors in Pass Christian about her husband and his accomplishments, my knees were shaking with the emotion of the day.

"I have one more thing for you," I said at the close of the ceremony. This was the first time Mark Michael of Naples, Florida had made pens from the cuttings of a Katrina sculpture. We presented the pens from that eagle tree in engraved rosewood boxes to the Roberts family and sent some with Robin to Diane Sawyer and Charlie Gibson at Good Morning America.

We followed the ceremony with lunch at Shaggy's. It's just hard to find a day better than that.

Marlin talking to Robin about her father's eagle.

General Touhill, Keesler AFB commander, spoke at the dedication ceremony. He also received a pen.

Afterwards, we had lunch at Shaggy's. In this picture : Nick, Alicia Gilbert, Mark Michael, Rene, Marlin, Teresa VanEps and Michael VanEps.

"It is fitting that this monument was carved at War Memorial Park. My father loved Mississippi. He loved Pass Christian. He loved the United States of America."

- Robin Roberts

Anchor of ABC's "Good Morning America"

Tuskegee Airmen

The Tuskegee Airmen were the first African American pilots in the United States.

They flew with such distinction during World War II, they earned more than 850 medals and were credited with shooting down 260 enemy planes as they flew protection for bomber squadrons during daylight raids over Germany.

The Tuskegee Airmen were trained near Tuskegee Institute in Alabama and at Keesler Air Force Base in Biloxi. By 1943, more than 7,000 African American soldiers and airmen were stationed on the Mississippi Gulf Coast.

Colonel Roberts joined the Army Air Corps at Keesler Field in 1943 and was assigned to the Tuskegee Airman pilot program in 1944. He retired as the commander of the maintenance and supply group at Keesler Air Force Base, where his career began 32 years before.

This large stainless plaque is on display at the base of the "Roberts Eagle" in War Memorial Park in Pass Christian.

American Idol singer Ace Young with Marlin.

War Memorial Park

Many towns across America have a gathering place for a Sunday jazz concert, art festivals and barbecues. In Pass Christian, that place is War Memorial Park.

Most of the Katrina sculptures I carved in South Mississippi are along Highway 90, which generally runs along the beach. War Memorial Park is elevated well above the road, giving stunning views of the water over the traffic.

The park has a history, and once you hear the story you can almost see President Teddy Roosevelt taking the path between the oaks to the water when he vacationed in Pass Christian in 1915.

The sculptures are a popular stop on the paths of the park.

The park is home to several military artifacts.

In memory of those who perished in the storm.

The park became one of my favorite places and I eventually carved four trees while the residents wandered in to watch me work. One woman particularly stands in my mind. She watched for a long time as I carved the smaller of two eagles in the park, and then told me how the eagle's gaze was in the direction of the home of her friend, who died during Hurricane Katrina.

Five years later, the Gulf oil spill in April 2010 tied the Katrina sculpture to another catastrophe on the Gulf Coast. Dolphins, turtles and fish floated up onto the beaches, and pelicans were found coated in oil. It reminded people, as the carvings do, that the marline life and birds that often get taken for granted are among Mississippi's greatest treasures.

An eagle watching over the park.

A large mother and baby humpback whale breaching 17' into the air.

This parrot makes for a great "photo op" for kids playing in the park.

"These old oaks are 300 years old and they represent the roots of the coast. To have these dead trees carved reflects a sign of recovery and renewal. They help the people stay focused on going forward."

- Chipper McDermott

Mayor, City of Pass Christian

The CW production crew with Mayor Chipper McDermott and Marlin Miller at Shaggy's in Pass Christian.

NBC Nightly News with Brian Williams

Ospreys and Whale Tail

The biggest and oldest tree in the chain of Katrina sculptures also had the most drama surrounding it. The ospreys and whale's tail was the sculpture that convinced everyone, including my wife and daughter, that I am truly crazy.

The first trees I carved in Biloxi were big enough for an owl here and a seahorse there. This tree was so old and massive it could become a multi-layered sculpture.

The problem was it stood very close to Highway 90 and therefore was marked for removal.

Because of the popularity of the other sculptures, the Mississippi Department of Transportation relented and I quickly got in there and carved the whale's tail on the portion of the tree that reached toward the water. That way I knew the tree would be safe from demolition.

What certified me as being crazy was while others were evacuating as Hurricane Gustav aimed at the Gulf Coast in September 2008, I chose that weekend to start carving the part of the trunk toward the highway.

The before picture.

This giant oak was over 7' across at the base. Marlin's mom Bonnie is dwarfed by it.

With the wind picking up and rain bands just starting to reach the Coast, I was hanging upside down in an out-stretched manlift with a chainsaw carving into the oak. Cars and vans packed for evacuation sped by, horns beeping. My wife, Rene, and daughter, Samantha, were with me that weekend and they said I was crazy, too.

Hurricanes are part of the cycle of life for South Mississippi. NBC Nightly News reporter Mark Potter came to Biloxi in 2005 to show the world the damage from Hurricane Katrina. Vincent Creel, Biloxi's public affairs officer, contacted Potter to see if he would return for the third anniversary to report on the Katrina sculptures.

Marlin taking a break to spend some time with his grandson, Bryce.

Marlin busy at work shaping the first osprey. He used over 50 chains, 6 carving bars, and 4 chainsaws to create this masterpiece.

Potter said this was the only time he ever presented a story to his producers and they instantly said yes, absolutely, go for it.

We decided we would build the completion of this sculpture around NBC Nightly News and scheduled it for January 2009. Cliff, the camera man, arrived in Biloxi the day before to shoot some footage.

"This has been the craziest ride for me over the last year," I told Cliff as the camera rolled. "Every five to six hours some car will stop, somebody will get out and they'll come up and tell me what it's meant to them or the kind of emotion this has brought out in them from what they endured in the storm. This is the most incredible emotional thing I've ever gone through," I said.

He looked at me like I was crazy. Then not five minutes later this lady stops her car and crosses the busy highway to come talk to me.

"You brought sunshine where there was none," she said, started to cry, while Cliff captured her words and emotion on camera.

"They love this stuff in New York," Cliff said.

NBC correspondent, Mark Potter, interviewing Marlin for the NBC Nightly News feature.

Sculptor Marlin Miller with Public Affairs Manager Vincent Creel and NBC's Mark Potter.

After 11 hours of shooting, much of the footage was edited out, but this entire episode with the woman was included in the final piece. It also made it onto the report when Potter came to our house at Fort Walton Beach, Florida and filmed a video with us during the Gulf oil spill.

For me that is what this whole thing was about: that lady and her emotions at that moment.

There was plenty more drama to film. Biloxi Mayor A.J. Holloway and his wife, Macklyn, swung by so Potter could interview him about the sculptures. The mayor didn't tell anyone he was on his way to the hospital. About 10 minutes after his NBC interview he was in intensive care, on his way to emergency surgery. I still tell him, "Mayor Holloway, you're the toughest guy I know."

Cameraman Cliff with Marlin and the huge "action cam chainsaw."

ABC's Krystal Allan also reporting on this sculpture project.

Waving for the camera.

The tree is in a high profile location, right next to the highway and beach, and I never had so many people just pull up a blanket and watch me carve. Of course, I wasn't getting much work done with the cameras and the onlookers. In the crowd was Randy Swanson, who owns Swanson Hardware Store in my small hometown of Manson, Iowa. He heard about the sculptures and stopped by on his vacation to see them. I was in his store only a few months earlier, buying a part to fix the ceiling fan at my mom's home, but we officially met in Biloxi.

Marlin and son, Preston, adding detail to the sculpture.

Hundreds of onlookers gathered near the seahorse sculpture throughout the weekend, a safe distance from the work in progress. They also enjoyed watching the many television crews that set up for the story.

NBC Nightly News aired this story in over 10,000,000 households on Easter Weekend 2009. It also aired on The Today Show and MSNBC.

An aerial view from 40' up looking down on the large osprey hanging over the highway.

The drama continued as we waited for the national debut of the Katrina sculptures. The feature would close NBC Nightly News, but four or five weeks running, golf tournaments kept going long and the news was shortened. I'd call family and friends to remind them to watch, then call them back to say it wouldn't be on. My poor mom must have thought it was all a lie.

Finally at the end of the golf season 10 million households saw the Katrina sculptures. The video made me realize what I called a token gesture of thanks to the people of Biloxi was maybe something more and the impact was large. The feature started with Mark Potter talking about the storm and how Katrina killed the trees. Then the camera pulls back and Mark is seen between osprey wings. It was a dramatic report and put the spotlight back on the Mississippi Gulf Coast.

Aerial view of the osprey sculpture.

This perched osprey is well over 30' in the air.

"From the goodness of his heart, and on his own time, Marlin Miller created a wonderful gift to the survivors of Hurricane Katrina. Drive along the Mississippi coast someday and try hard not to smile when his tree sculptures come into view. You won't succeed. That's the beauty of Marlin Miller's gift."

- Mark Potter

NBC News

Breathing New Life

Trees that stood along the beach in Biloxi for generations couldn't withstand Hurricane Katrina's saltwater storm surge. When leaves stopped growing and the trees died, they were marked with a big red R for removal.

When I first started carving the trees, I felt a rush to keep ahead of the highway crews. As I completed a trail of sculptures and their popularity grew, I felt more assured the trees wouldn't be chopped by them but carved by me.

During a couple of fall weekends I sculpted a pair of cypress trees into a heron and a pelican perched on a pier, as they often are along the coastline.

Come spring I got an unexpected phone call from Vincent Creel, who handles public relations for the City of Biloxi.

The dead cypress trees were showing life, he said, sending out branches and vivid greenery. The trees are very close to the eastbound lanes of Highway 90 and are hard to miss, especially with feathery green leaves sprouting against the reddish brown wood.

"We're coming back, and this is one of the things that is helping us do that."

- A.J. Holloway
Mayor , City of Biloxi

Some people were concerned the trees were carved prematurely. Others worried the branches would grow around the sculpture and obscure the carving. Biloxi Mayor A.J. Holloway dismissed the controversy, saying the trees were marked for removal and would be gone if not for the carvings, and the green branches were simply the birds' nests.

Walt Grayson, who hosts "Mississippi Roads" for public television was captivated by the story of the cypress carvings showing new life. He filmed a segment with these trees and at the Institute of Marine Mammal Studies in Gulfport.

The pelican cypress eventually stopped producing any branches, but the heron still sits on his green nest four years later.

"What Marlin has done for this community is just a Godsend. It's a gift that's going to give for generations."

- Vincent Creel
City of Biloxi Public
Affairs Manager

LONG BEACH SCULPTURES

It's been a long road back for the City of Long Beach, which was smashed so hard by Hurricane Katrina.

When Long Beach Alderman Richard Burton saw the trees I carved in nearby Biloxi, he tracked me down and asked how much it would cost to carve one or two of the big oak trees that were standing dead in the median of Hwy 90 in his city. He was certain my tree carvings would reassure Long Beach residents that something good could come from the destruction.

The city couldn't afford much, he told me. Hurricane Katrina wiped out so many homes and businesses and Long Beach, like the other cities across South Mississippi, had huge expenses and a slim tax base after the storm.

It wasn't his movie star name but his determination that struck me, and I told him I would carve the trees at no charge to the city.

This was my first venture toward the western coast of Mississippi and the response from the community was just incredible. So many people came up to talk with me that I started arriving very early in the morning to get work done.

Sculptor Marlin Miller was busy at work as the construction crews repaired the beaches and highways that were devastated by Hurricane Katrina.

I was sitting in my truck in the grass median at 3 am, waiting for enough light to begin carving the tree, when a Long Beach police officer drove up and asked what I was doing there. The next early morning, I decided to wait for daylight in the nearby Burger King parking lot, thinking nobody was around. The manager happened to be there very early and called the police. A different officer responded and I reassured him of my purpose there by pulling out a newspaper article with a picture of me carving. We talked until the sun came up.

On the west side of town I coaxed a pod of dolphins out of a tall tree with tall, reaching branches. On the east side of Long Beach, a large tree gave me the canvas to carve two sea turtles, an eagle and anhinga birds, which are natives to Southern marshlands and are known to fluff out their feathers when they get wet.

I still often get emails from the people I've met in Long Beach and whenever I'm in town, the police come by to say hello, now that they know I belong in their city even early in the morning.

Marlin working on a hot day adding detail to a pod of dolphins.

Marlin preparing the anhinga/sea turtle tree for varnish.

I've found all kinds of things in the trees I've carved, and in the oak on the east end of Long Beach black widow spiders stood guard over a treasure.

This was the first time my son, Preston Miller, then 15, helped me with a carving. After I relocated the spiders out of our range, we found a canister in a knothole in the tree. Inside was a small flashlight and instead of batteries we discovered a message with map coordinates. One day Preston and I will grab our GPS and set out on a treasure hunt to find that treasure of the tree.

Preston helping his dad put the finishing touches on a sculpture.

Marlin started his carving days as early as 5:00 am.

USM GOLDEN EAGLES
Gulf Park Campus

Long Beach Alderman Richard Burton all along had his eyes on a pair of huge oaks across from the front entrance to the University of Southern Mississippi. The mascots are the Southern Miss Golden Eagles and Burton could see eagles in the branches.

I could see them, too, along with the struggle ahead to transform the massive trees into graceful eagle carvings. One tree grew out of the bank between the four-lane Hwy 90 and was very close to the road.

The challenge came right from the start, when I topped the tree at night so I could see oncoming headlights. That way I could estimate how much time I had to slice through the branches, watch them smash onto the road, jump down, cut them into manageable sections and move the wood off the road. I had this scramble going on and a couple of times I was probably in the drivers' headlights by the time the road was clear. In hindsight I could have asked the agreeable Long Beach Police for some assistance.

On a foggy morning, sculptor Marlin Miller gave shape to the wings of an eagle.

Tourists taking pictures of the famous eagles.

The tree is shaped like a twisted Y and the first eagle I carved flies off the grassy bank at an angle, with one wing coming out of the ground and the other reaching 17 feet into the sky. The eagle looks like it's cruising down the highway or is an airplane approaching a landing strip. The second section of the tree is an eagle facing out, looking with the traffic.

"I knew what it was going to be", Long Beach Mayor Billy Skellie told me when he dropped by as I worked. "I saw it weeks before you started carving."

This carving brought a whole other group out to watch the progress - the USM alumni - who told me in person and with hundreds of emails how delighted they are to have their mascot flying in front of the campus.

Several coats of marine varnish made the eagles truly golden and soar to life.

As a keepsake, I supplied a chunk of oak from the Golden Eagle tree and Mark Michael from Naples, Florida made it into a pen for USM President, Dr. Martha Saunders.

The eagles were dedicated in a ceremony at the Gulf campus and I was presented a plaque in thanks from the university. Equally gratifying was a photograph of the eagles which graced the main page of the USM website for the next six months.

From left to right, artist Marlin Miller, Long Beach Mayor Billy Skellie, Southern Miss Gulf Coast Associate Provost Pat Joachim and Southern Miss Provost Bob Lyman pose next to the sculpture of golden eagles in front of the university's Gulf Park campus in Long Beach.

Gulf Park Campus History

The 100th birthday of the University of Southern Mississippi in 2010 gave students, faculty and alumni the opportunity to look back at the history of the college and ahead to the university's "golden" future.

Quarterback Brett Favre and singer, songwriter, author Jimmy Buffett are among the most famous USM alumni. The main campus in Hattiesburg opened in 1910 as a teaching college and the first classes on the Gulf Coast were in 1947 in Biloxi.

What was the Gulf Park College for Women on Highway 90 in Long Beach became the Gulf Park Campus of the University of Southern Mississippi in 1972. The campus is directly across the highway from the beaches of the Gulf of Mexico and Katrina roared in and left $115 million in damage. Five years later the campus is still being rebuilt and the university responds to another disaster, as the Gulf oil spill brings tar balls and oil sheen to the shore.

USM and its Gulf Coast Research Lab in Ocean Springs are among the leading academic institutions in the country studying the effects of Hurricane Katrina and the Gulf oil spill on the local environment.

Construction continues 5 years after the destruction of Katrina.

GULF PARK COLLEGE

Founded 1921 by Colonel J. C. Hardy Gulf Park College provided unique educational experiences for young women at the secondary and junior college level. The college enjoyed fifty years of operation as an educational institution filled with grace, culture, charm and tradition. It operated successfully until 1971 when the sagging economy, damage from Hurricane Camille, and the upswing of low cost community colleges forced it to close. THE UNIVERSITY OF SOUTHERN MISSISSIPPI began operation on the campus in 1972. Today Southern Miss offers undergraduate and graduate programs at this site.

ERECTED 2003
BY LONG BEACH HISTORICAL SOCIETY AND THE UNIVERSITY OF SOUTHERN MISSISSIPPI

"The University is truly honored to have these magnificent eagles soaring over the front of our Gulf Park Campus. They are a symbol of strength and endurance, reminding us of where we have been and inspiring us to reach for new heights."

_ Sheila White, M.Ed.

Director, University Communications

The University of Southern Mississippi Gulf Coast

Friendship Oak

Gulf Park Campus

When Hurricane Katrina tore apart the Mississippi Gulf Coast, residents didn't know how extensive the damage was. They only knew it was bad. After they checked on their homes and neighbors, one of the first questions they asked was, "Did the Friendship Oak survive?"

The huge live oak tree has stood near the entrance to the Gulf Park Campus of the University of Southern Mississippi since 1487 - before Columbus set sail - and has survived many a storm. The tree stands 50 feet tall and its lower branches, heavy with girth and age, rest on the ground.

The nearby buildings were badly damaged or destroyed by Katrina, but the Friendship Oak lives on.

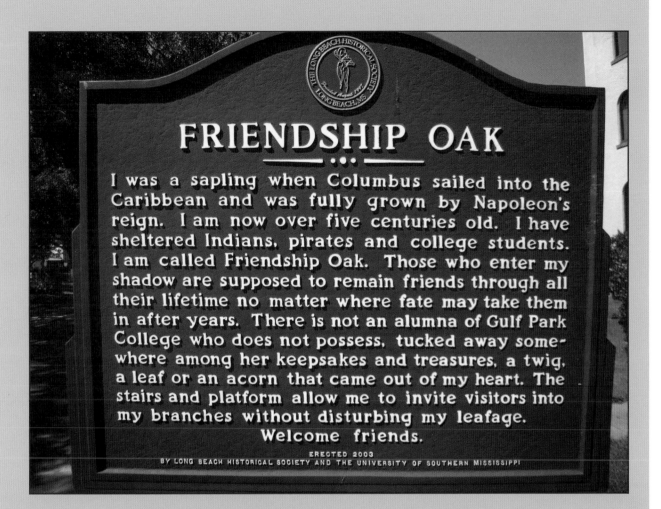

FRIENDSHIP OAK

I was a sapling when Columbus sailed into the Caribbean and was fully grown by Napoleon's reign. I am now over five centuries old. I have sheltered Indians, pirates and college students. I am called Friendship Oak. Those who enter my shadow are supposed to remain friends through all their lifetime no matter where fate may take them in after years. There is not an alumna of Gulf Park College who does not possess, tucked away somewhere among her keepsakes and treasures, a twig, a leaf or an acorn that came out of my heart. The stairs and platform allow me to invite visitors into my branches without disturbing my leafage. Welcome friends.

ERECTED 2003
BY LONG BEACH HISTORICAL SOCIETY AND THE UNIVERSITY OF SOUTHERN MISSISSIPPI

The massive oaks on the Mississippi Gulf Coast are full of history. Oh, the stories they could tell.

"Two weeks into my first public service term as Alderman in Long Beach , Katrina hit us. The live oaks destroyed by Katrina were an important part of our identity on the coast. I noticed other cities being blessed with your carvings and decided to contact you. From that meeting on Christmas Eve morning came 3 carvings for our city. When I talked to you on the phone I mentioned one tree, but when we met I hopefully mentioned 2 others and you accepted the challenge right away. When I told Mayor Billy Skellie that Long Beach would have its own carvings he replied: "Who's going to pay for it?" I said: "Marlin Miller is donating the work." The mayor said: "Well bless you son." That's the nicest thing he ever said to me.

Your sculptures transformed our dead trees from sad reminders of what we lost to uplifting works of art. The centuries old oak that was killed by Katrina in front of the University of Southern Mississippi in Long Beach was a good candidate for carving even though MDOT planned to remove it. I felt it was important to try to have it carved into Eagles, their mascot. That and the others along Beach Boulevard all turned out beautifully. Now the sculptures are our number one tourist attraction. Every time I pass the Eagles I remember what we all went through and how we stuck together and persevered."

Thanks Marlin for your carvings, they mean a lot to us.

- Richard Burton

Alderman Ward 3 Long Beach, Mississippi 2005-2009

Ohr Museum

The Ohr O'Keefe Museum of Art in Biloxi was only a year from opening when Hurricane Katrina dealt it an unlucky hand, washing a casino barge from its moorings and dropping it on the construction site.

The highly collectible work of "the mad potter" George Ohr was saved, but with all the expenses after the storm, there was a question if the museum could come back.

The museum board started fundraisers to get the money needed to repair the buildings designed by famed architect Frank Gehry.

I participated in the annual Ohr festival of arts held at the Biloxi Town Green and donated two sculptures, a bird and an eagle, which helped fill the museum bank account when they were sold at the Ohr gala at the Beau Rivage Resort and Casino.

The directors also asked me to participate in a Doors for Ohr fundraising promotion that would help raise the needed funds to open the museum. About 50 artists were asked to contribute an actual door made in their medium. The doors will be auctioned to raise money and featured in a book that also will add to the fund.

The first buildings opened on Nov. 6, 2010 are the Mississippi Sound Welcome Center, the IP Casino Resort Exhibitions Gallery and the Gallery of African American Art.

This long-awaited opening of the $36 million museum complex brings more recognition to Ohr's multicolored glazed pottery and also to Biloxi.

Frank Gehry won a Pulitzer Prize for architecture and was named "the most important architect of our age" by Vanity Fair. His designs for the Guggenheim Museum in Bilbao, Spain and others around the world are tourist attractions in themselves.

This "old" 70 pound pine door is a relief replica of the view and sculpture on the Town Green. It is called "Ohr's View." This is one of several sculptures Marlin has donated to raise money for the museum.

Stone County

Seventy miles of the Mississippi Coast were flattened by Hurricane Katrina's storm surge and the wind damage extended more than twice that far inland. Tornados and high winds from the storm twisted off roofs, toppled trees and left behind piles of wood where homes once stood.

In the devastation along the Coast, Stone County, 30 miles north of Gulfport was "The Lost County." There were some volunteers, including a group of Methodist men from Michigan that came to help and five years later are still returning to rebuild the area, but it was up to the residents to find the vision and strength to rebuild.

Kathryn Lewis, a retired teacher at Mississippi Gulf Coast Community College, wasn't about to let Stone County be forgotten. She appointed herself the head of the Telling Trees Project and set out to create art that would bring visitors to the area and make a lasting impression on the residents.

She found me working at the Little Children's Park in Ocean Springs and convinced me to carve a perched eagle glancing at the historic courthouse in Wiggins.

A row of pecan trees lead to the beautiful courthouse and the pecan I carved was a good size tree in the garden off to one side. While I carved, Kathryn shuttled my daughter, Samantha, and her friends to the nearby Flint Creek Water Park and on to McDonald's when it started to rain.

Several of the county supervisors stopped by to see the progress and jumped into their cars when the weather turned mean. I worked in and out of the lightening to finish the eagle and inmates from the local prison came in after I carved and cleaned up the scraps of wood. It was full community participation on this carving.

Marlin as he finishes the eagle preparing it for it's new life looking over the Stone County Court-house.

Much of the energy after Hurricane Katrina went to rebuild the Coast so Kathryn Lewis took up the charge for Stone County.

"I'm a retired teacher who loves where I live," she said. That was her inspiration for the Telling Trees Project that celebrates the community and tells its history through murals and woodcarvings.

Stone County is becoming an eco-tourism area, where visitors come in and spend a day on the farm. They also take a tour of the murals found in schools and parks throughout the area, and they stop to see the eagle carving.

Lewis said the Marlin Miller eagle makes a connection with Stone County, celebrating the resilience of the residents and the ecosystem.

Wiggins is a small Southern town full of people with such good spirit. I really enjoyed my time there. Before we left, Kathryn presented us with a gift basket of personal items made by Wiggins' craftsmen. In the assortment were a painted planter, ceramic mugs and a Christmas tree ornament that hangs on the dash of my pickup truck. Every day when the sun hits the angel made of pine straw needles, it casts an angel shadow across the dash board of the truck. That angel means more to me than you know.

D'Iberville Redfish Cup

ESPN announcer interviewing Marlin at the Redfish Cup finals.

Sculptor Marlin Miller presenting trophies to the champions.

Anglers showing off their catch.

The Mississippi Gulf Coast attracts many of the top fishing tournaments in the country. During the fourth anniversary of Hurricane Katrina in August 2009, fishermen from across the South came to try their luck at winning the Redfish Cup.

Hosting the world-class event, considered to be the nation's premier saltwater fishing series, was the City of D'Iberville. I am always asked to do carvings for special events and since I hadn't done any carvings in the city, I agreed to create team trophies and a large redfish for the series.

This was the final competition in the series leading up to the championship and ESPN camera crews were taping the event to air on ESPN 2 later in the year. Reporters and photographers from several other sports media were jockeying for the best story and picture while the 50-plus teams of fishermen were casting for the biggest fish. I carved all day. When the boats returned to weigh in, I helped present the redfish trophy I created to the winning team. The producer of the show caught the whopper, the great big redfish I'd carved.

Marlin's wife , Rene, putting the final touches on the trophies at the Redfish Cup.

"I work for the National Wildlife Federation and already knew about your post Katrina tree sculptures. All of us here have been worried to death while reporting on oiled species and other environmental problems in the Gulf. Sources of inspiration, such as your work, are so very welcome and encouraging.

- Kevin Coyle

National Wildlife Federation

Thanks goes out to Stihl Corporation for supporting the community events.

An angler and his family posing for a picture with sculptor Marlin Miller.

Redfish Cup winners with their trophies and the sculptor in the courtesy tent.

City of D'Iberville

Mayor Rusty Quave was at the D'Iberville pier much of the time and I was struck by his enthusiasm for his city. It is the smallest of 11 cities in South Mississippi and is inland from the coast, with its shores on the Back Bay of Biloxi. It's also at the intersection of two major highways, interstates 10 and 110. Since Katrina a major shopping center was built and people wanting to get away from any future hurricane wind and storm surge moved to D'Iberville.

It was also chosen for the site for the Ocean Expo, a sea life experience that will be built and operated by my friend, Dr. Moby Solangi, and his staff at the Institute for Marine Mammal Studies. They eventually plan to connect this attraction with a boat ride to the IMMS so visitors will have fun and understand the importance of protecting the dolphins and other mammals in the Gulf.

Mark Michael and sculptor Marlin Miller presenting Mayor Quave with an oak pen made from a Katrina sculpture.

Marlin and Rene with Dr. Moby Solangi at the Marine Mammal Institute.

Keep America Beautiful's
GREAT AMERICAN CLEANUP

The tree carvings started purely as a way to salute the recovery of Biloxi after Hurricane Katrina but soon branched out to other areas and interests.

Waveland, on the most westerly coast in Mississippi, was chosen as the site of the national kickoff of the Great American Cleanup (GAC) campaign in 2009 for the Keep America Beautiful organization. Mayor Tommy Longo called me at my studio in Florida to ask if I would do a carving for the event and the city. Waveland was "Ground Zero" for Hurricane Katrina and Longo talked about what he and his city had survived. City employee Joy Normand and I went searching Waveland for the right tree to carve. So many of the trees were toppled by Katrina and we found only three dead standing trees that might work. The largest was a pine just 10 inches in diameter, and I left Waveland thinking the project wasn't going to happen.

Then it came to me – let's plant a big dead tree on the busiest corner in the city, at the intersection of Highways 90 and 603. It was just two weeks until the event and we needed permission from the Mississippi Department of Transportation, heavy equipment and Mayor Longo's can-do attitude to make it happen.

Longo asked his friend Chipper McDermott, the mayor of nearby Pass Christian, to be on the lookout for a big tree. Pass Christian Police Chief John Dubuisson found it - at least 10 tons of a tree - and a crew brought it on a flatbed trailer. A big crane and the city's backhoe were used to move it. As they attempted to lift the massive log off the truck, the weight flipped the city's backhoe, smashing the window and knocking the wind out of the driver, who proved to be otherwise ok.

Meanwhile, I was in a man lift carving a sculpture in Pass Christian when I heard about the tree vs. backhoe. With faith in the crew, I kept working while they heaved the tree off the trailer with one of the big cranes. The tree was planted and cemented into place at the Waveland intersection.

Only a "Crazy Yankee" would plant a dead tree, Waveland employees said as I went to work carving the tree. I had the support of the community. Never had I heard so many horns honk at me in my life. It was every minute, constantly, as I worked.

I was still at it after 10 pm that first cold, windy night. The next morning they could see I had found a sculpture in the wood like none other I had done.

Emerging from the wood were three playful dolphins and a sea turtle with his fins and head hanging off the log. After working all the next day and another, the sculpture was complete.

Across the city 1,000 volunteers, including students on a working spring break from Loyola University, Maryland, were helping Keep America Beautiful by picking up litter and planting flowers and trees.

Waveland is the gateway to Mississippi on US 90 coming from Louisiana, and the sculpture is one of the first things visitors see. My stepson, Allen Leonard, helped me varnish it, providing the finishing touch that makes it pop among the traffic.

Allen adding the final touches.

GREAT AMERICAN CLEANUP
Pass Christian

In 2010, The Great American Cleanup kickoff was back in South Mississippi for the fifth time since Hurricane Katrina - this time at Pass Christian.

Gail Cunningham, Keep America Beautiful managing director and the head of Great American Cleanup, asked if I would contribute another sculpture. I volunteered to carve a parrot in War Memorial Park, where I had already completed three carvings.

Joining Pass Christian Mayor Chipper McDermott at the kickoff were the mayors of the cities that had hosted the previous four events: Mayor A.J. Holloway of Biloxi, Mayor George Schloegel of Gulfport, Mayor Billy Skellie of Long Beach and Mayor Tommy Longo of Waveland.

Keep America Beautiful President Matt McKenna also was there, along with Miss America 2010 Caressa Cameron, who beautified the city and inspired the volunteers.

Gail Cunningham recalled the thousands of volunteers who transformed the South Mississippi Coast since Katrina.

The Pass Christian event brought together students on spring break from DePaul University in Alabama and Auburn University in Alabama, airmen from Keesler Air Force Base in Biloxi, the local Scouts, the garden club and business people who each did their part to Keep America Beautiful.

Mayor Longo, Mayor Skellie, Mayor Holloway, Miss America 2010 Caressa Cameron, Mayor McDermott and Gail Cunningham with Sculptor Marlin Miller and other members of the kickoff crew.

"Marlin Miller has been a key member of Keep America Beautiful's Great American Cleanup Project team since our public space restoration and beautification activities on the Mississippi Gulf Coast began soon after Hurricane Katrina. His love of the area, his passion for volunteering and his imagination and creative hand have brought scores of the once regal oaks back to life in the form of graceful sculptures. He has created beauty and art where there was once destruction, and thanks to his amazing talent there are now majestic centerpieces along Highway 90 for all to enjoy and celebrate."

— Gail Cunningham, Senior Vice President, Keep America Beautiful, Inc. and Managing Director, Great American Cleanup

Sculptor Marlin Miller with Gail Cunningham at Pass Christian's "Great American Cleanup" kickoff.

Sculptor Marlin Miller making progress on Waveland's "gateway" sculpture.

Marlin setting the eyes on a parrot in War Memorial Park.

Marlin sharing the stage with Miss America 2010 Caressa Cameron at the kickoff of the "Great American Cleanup" in Pass Christian.

About Keep America Beautiful

From her home on the shores of Connecticut, Gail Cunningham saw Katrina aiming for the Gulf Coast and knew the devastation the hurricane would leave in it's path.

The senior vice president of Keep America Beautiful and the managing director of its Great American Cleanup, Cunningham had been through hurricanes, but none with the intensity of Katrina. Her family lived on the water in Connecticut for 90 years and she learned about the flood mitigation, preparedness and restoration after a storm. "It was just a part of my DNA," she said.

With the assistance of Barbara Dorr, the Mississippi director of Keep America Beautiful, she was on the Coast within a month after the storm. For the next five years, with the help of dozens of sponsors, she would oversee the greatest of Great American Cleanup projects in five cities across South Mississippi.

Great American Cleanup is the nation's largest community improvement program, with 30,000 events each year all across the United States between March 1 and May 31.

Volunteers and community members gearing up for a day of beautifying Pass Christian.

2006 - The Biloxi Town Green was the national kickoff for GAC. "People in Mississippi don't wait for you to come do it for them," Cunningham said. "There were a good 1,000 people who turned up that morning," including airmen from Keesler Air Force Base and the Navy Seabees from Gulfport. Yates Construction Company helped rebuild the raised shoofly - a circular deck around a huge oak tree. The volunteers also restored the Purple Heart memorial in the nearby Henry Beck Park.

2007 - West Side Park in Gulfport was an ambitious project on 10 acres plus beach. Cunningham worried there wouldn't be enough people to do the work, when over the knoll came teams of volunteers and 300 students in matching T - shirts from West Elementary School. A shoofly and splash pad were later added to the park.

2008 - Long Beach, just west of Gulfport, had considerable damage from Katrina and KAB transformed four sites. They built gazebos and picnic tables, planted flowers and trees and cleaned up litter and debris.

2009 - Waveland saw volunteers from as far away as the Netherlands and Mexico helping clean and restore 11 sites. Rows of graceful palms were planted at the entrance to Veterans Memorial Park and the fountain was working again by the end of the day when the Veterans of Foreign Wars arrived to play Taps.

2010 - Pass Christian had 8 sites improved. "We left the harbor looking amazing," she said, and a Marlin Miller sculpture in the park is a remembrance of the day.

"Marlin has been a shining star," she said. "I can look at a park and envision what it will be. He can look at a tree and see a beautiful sculpture." Together the trail of sculptures tells the story of the area and the treasured wildlife, she said.

Pallets of sod and hundreds of plants awaiting their final destination.

Ocean Springs

Ocean Springs was hurt by Katrina, but less so than some of the other cities on the Mississippi Gulf Coast.

Artists are drawn to Ocean Springs and its gracious downtown, shaded by centuries old oak trees. Several times a year festivals fill the streets and parks.

It was at the Herb and Garden festival that Mayor Connie Moran came to our booth and asked if I would do a carving for the city. All of the oak trees destroyed by the storm were cleared away quickly and it was a challenge to find a tree to carve in a public place. Finally, we found a smooth, elongated pecan tree in the Little Children's Park off Washington Avenue, just beyond the downtown shopping area.

The people here love their live oak trees. The oaks that survived the storm are cherished and protected. Note the clearance sign attached to the lower branch of this large oak located on Washington Avenue.

Little Children's Park

Many people don't even know the carving is there because it isn't visible from the street. You have to get out of the car and walk into the park to see the families with young children playing beneath it every day.

The tree is narrow at the top and opens up at the base. Like the moms and children playing around the tree, I could see a mama dolphin with a pod of babies swimming above her. The weekend I carved there were at least five or six birthday parties in the park and I provided entertainment for them.

This is one of the tallest sculptures I've carved and we had to take down the fence to bring in the man lift so I could get to the upper reaches of the tree. It was a windy day and I could feel the man lift wobbling as I carved with the chainsaw.

The dead pecan tree before it was carved.

Looking straight up at the finished sculpture, which is

nearly three stories tall.

When I told my teenage daughter, Samantha, that it felt at times like I was going to be blown over, she laughed and teased that her dad was afraid to go up high. The next morning the wind was still blowing and I gave her a ride in the man lift to the top of the tree. Like the families on the playground, I had to have a little fun with her. "Look at the leg on the lift," I told her. "It looks like it's coming off the ground and this whole thing is going to tip over." I'd been in the lift all the previous day so I knew it was safe, but her eyes got big, her knuckles got white as she gripped the safety bar. She was ready to get back on the ground. It wasn't her kind of playground ride and I joked with her, "Don't you ever say anything bad about your father again."

Dolphin pod sculpture located in Little Children's Park.

"Marlin's sculptures were a true inspiration to all of us during the months and years after Katrina. Amidst all of the destruction, his work would lighten our burden as we rebuilt."

- Gene Taylor

U.S. Congressman

Institute for Marine Mammal Studies

The people I've met while carving the Katrina sculptures are what stands out most in my mind. I've met residents who came home after Hurricane Katrina and found nothing, leaders who stepped up to rebuild hope and their communities and celebrities who came to support the Mississippi Gulf Coast.

And I met a team at the Institute for Marine Mammal Studies in Gulfport whose compassion for the dolphins and turtles they rescue just drew me into a project for them.

Dr. Moby Solangi founded the Institute in 1984 to care for stranded dolphins and research their habitat on the Gulf Coast, where most of the world's bottlenose dolphins live. He is assisted by people like Delphine Vanderpool, a medical doctor from California who instead of caring for humans came to Mississippi and devoted her skills to the dolphins.

Marlin was given a tour by the Marine Mammal Institute staff.

About 15 members of this amazing staff accompanied me on the tour of the facility. The thing I remember most was when we watched the video about the rescue of the Katrina dolphins. After all the times the staff had seen it, there wasn't a dry eye in the theater. You could just feel the spirit and the commitment to that project.

In 2009, I was contacted by producer Key Ivy about filming a segment for the television show Mississippi Roads on PBS. I didn't know he was at the dedication of the eagle for Col. Roberts in Pass Christian and that he already had film of me with Robin Roberts and her family.

I told him about the three playful dolphins I was preparing to carve at the IMMS and that became the focus of the show with Mississippi Roads host Walt Grayson. With time-lapse photography they videotaped the entire process as I carved the trio of dolphins leaping into the air. After three days of taping the combined images had me looking like I was drinking too much coffee.

Marlin sizing up the three large logs.

The initial cuts are made.

The logs begin to take shape.

The Mississippi Roads segment continues to be seen in the displays at the Gulfport-Biloxi International Airport and the Mississippi Welcome Center on Interstate 10.

I was invited back to IMMS for a party in December 2009 and brought my kids, Samantha and Preston, and my grandson, Bryce Leonard, then 4. We got to see the dolphin that was on the Today Show and peak in the necropsy building to see an autopsy of a dolphin in progress.

As a gift to the IMMS staff, I carved a wall hanging of the eight Katrina dolphins whose story was featured on the Larry King show and by so much of the national media.

Moby said the dolphins in the rose garden at IMMS are a big hit with school groups who come to tour the center as I did, handle shark teeth and learn how the staff cares for the dolphins.

IMMS is preparing to extend its reach by building an Ocean Expo aquarium and dolphin experience in nearby D'Iberville.

Doing detail work on the last of three dolphins.

Allen and Bryce Leonard preparing to see the Today Show dolphin.

*The dolphins are now ready for
their varnish finish.*

*Rene with the finished dolphins in their new
home in the rose garden.*

The education center has a full display of sea life models and hands-on activities.

Marlin viewing a "dolphin recovery system" inside the media center.

The IMMS is a popular place for school and youth group field trips. The "shark tooth" and "touch tank" displays are especially popular with the young visitors.

"Marlin Miller has offered hope in the face of despair, beauty in the face of ruin and painted a bright silver lining in dark ominous clouds that hung over the Mississippi Gulf Coast. His simple gesture of turning Katrina damaged trees to wondrous works of art has spread into a movement that has become larger than anyone could have imagined. His countless hours of dedication and hard work are evident all along the coast in the form of the magnificent wood sculptures that were created with a chainsaw."

- Key Ivy

Director/Producer, Mississippi Public Broadcasting

KATRINA DOLPHINS

When Hurricane Katrina roared onshore in August 2005, it left many thousands of South Mississippi residents and eight dolphins homeless.

The Marine Life Oceanarium was on the waterfront in Gulfport and little was left when Katrina's storm surge subsided, including the eight dolphins. Some of the animals were evacuated before the storm hit, but the bottlenose dolphins were swept out of their steel reinforced concrete tank and into the sea along with buildings and houses.

Shannon Huyser training the famous Katrina Dolphins in the wild environment.

Marcy Romagnoli and Tim Hoffland with the Katrina Dolphins.

Dr. Moby Solangi, president of the Marine Life Oceanarium in Gulfport and now the director of the Institute for Marine Mammal Studies, said the dolphins were starving when their trainers found them in the Mississippi Sound. The water was filled with debris and toxic materials and Solangi knew they had to move them to a safe location or they would likely perish.

Tim Hoffland, Dr. Connie Chevis, Shannon Huyser and Marcy Romagnoli providing food and medicine to the stranded dolphins.

Shannon Huyser helping with the transport of an injured sea lion.

The story of the rescue was told by newspapers across the country and was seen on all the major television networks. Some of the dolphins had visible wounds when their trainers and expert volunteers went out to feed them medicine-laden fish throughout the day. The training whistles that taught the dolphins to do tricks were used to coax them onto floating mats that were lifted into the boat.

The dolphins initially were taken to facilities around the country for treatment before being reunited and flown to the Bahamas, where they were the first residents of Dolphin Cay at the Atlantis resort on Paradise Island.

Marcy Romagnoli and Shannon Huyser preparing the dolphins to be removed from the wild.

The eight Katrina Dolphins were swept from their tank during the hurricane. They survived for several days, miles from home, until they were rescued by their trainers. Their story was featured on the Larry King show. Marlin created this re-lief sculpture in honor of the dolphins. It now hangs in the administrative offices of the Institute.

IMMS Responds to the Oil Disaster

The Gulf oil spill in April 2010 happened 100 miles south of the Mississippi coast. Dolphins and turtles whose habitats were damaged or destroyed washed ashore before the oily tar balls.

Beach crews called the Institute for Marine Mammal Studies to pick up more than 200 animals, including 30 live sea turtles that were cared for at IMMS's turtle rehab center.

One of the turtles they recovered weighs more than 200 pounds and because her front fins are missing she won't be released back into the Gulf. She's staying at IMMS, where four people lift her every day to change the water in her tank.

Marlin inspecting a baby sea turtle.

This big girl lost both front flippers to a shark. She will remain at the institute where she is pampered.

I had the opportunity to tour the rehabilitation center with Mississippi First Lady Marsha Barbour and other officials and then release four of the Ridley turtles back into the sea.

Preparing a turtle for release.

A media boat followed our boat out to the entrance of the Gulf. The turtles, about the size of three dinner plates, wanted out of their plastic transport bins. We had our fingers on a pressure point on their head to keep them calm until they were released.

It was a great thing to see them swim away healthy and back at home.

Marlin with Marsha Barbour on the turtle release boat.

Marsha releases the last of the four turtles into the Gulf of Mexico.

Richard Murphy Hospice House

Most of the carvings stand along the beach, a reminder of the devastation of Hurricane Katrina and the marine life that remains. When people see reports of my work in the newspaper or on television, I get hundreds of requests to carve a tree or create a sculpture. Every once in a while I accept and the Richard Murphy Hospice in Hammond, Louisiana, was one of those times.

My brother, Dr. Michael Miller, had recently died of pancreatic cancer and my brother-in-law, John Webb, had also recently passed away from cancer. Hospice had cared for them to the end.

From the outside, the ranch house blends into the neighborhood. Step inside and it's just an incredible feeling to experience the calm. Beyond the glass patio doors in the living room is a meditation garden surrounding a tree in the compact back yard. Katrina took the life of the tree but not the spirit of the garden. This was the first time I branched out to do a carving in Louisiana. My daughter, Samantha Miller, 16 at the time, drove us the entire 5 hour trip from Florida. The calm of the garden was welcoming.

Sculptor Marlin Miller and his daughter,
Samantha, getting ready for their 250
mile Hospice House journey.

Marlin taking a moment to envision the sculpture within.

The eagle coming to life.

I could see the guardian eagle in the old oak, looking away from the house toward a future flight, taking shape in the tree before I even started.

On the hottest day of the year in June 2009, I went to work in the bright sun. Two of the three people being cared for in the home were well enough to watch from their wheelchairs. I could feel the connection with my brother and brother-in-law as I carved.

In the heat and humidity, sawdust covered my arms with each cut of the chainsaw and acted like insulation. At one point I became lightheaded and had to climb down from the tree and retreat to the comfort of the air conditioned home.

Local newspapers and television reporters came by to get the story. A visiting 6 year old, recognizing the serenity that Director Donna Landry has created in the home, spoke up and asked, "Why is everybody so nice here?"

As I drove us back home, Samantha and I spent the first hour reflecting on the day. We knew it was right. This was a really good thing.

"The garden is the last thing our patients see, so we wanted something really pretty there."

"When someone you love becomes a memory, the memory becomes a treasure. Thanks for making our dead oak tree a treasure."

- Donna Landry, Hospice House Director

Marlin had a chance to take a break from the heat and sawdust to visit with a patient. Several young visitors and journalists stopped by to say hello and see the artist at work.

About Richard Murphy Hospice House

When Richard Murphy learned he had terminal cancer, he wanted to spend his last days at home instead of in a hospital. His family, friends and medical team fulfilled his request by establishing the first hospice network in Hammond, Louisiana.

Since his death, the Richard Murphy Hospice Foundation has raised funds so those who don't have insurance will receive hospice care.

In 2006, the foundation opened the Richard Murphy Hospice House in a quiet neighborhood at the edge of historic Hammond. It is the first non-hospital owned hospice house in Louisiana.

Serving on the foundation's board of directors are community and business leaders who know firsthand of the "angel touch" of hospice staff who care for their terminally ill family members or friends.

Keesler Air Force Base

The first time I saw the Mississippi Gulf Coast was when I arrived at Keesler Air Force Base, and the trail of Katrina sculptures led me back to Biloxi and the base nearly three decades later.

It was 1981 and I was a punk kid from Manson, Iowa, straight out of high school, coming to Keesler for electronics school. That was the start of a great adventure in the Air Force that took me from Keesler to Hickman Air Force Base in Hawaii. There I was able to work full time in the Air Force, attend college full-time at Hawaii Pacific University and even surf a bit.

When an assignment came to go to Europe and work in special operations, taking our forces up to parachute out of planes, I jumped at it and re-enlisted. I had the best job - one that took me to places like Zaire, Morocco, Spain - 30 some countries in three years.

Thirty years later, after I had completed many of the Katrina sculptures on the beach in Biloxi, I got a call from Paula Strawn. Keesler wanted to commission me to carve a wood sculpture for the $65 million BX and Commissary opening in April 2010.

A film clip of the creation of the Keesler eagle...

I was really busy at the time, but Paula was persistent. "I want you to come and look at this facility," she said.

Hurricane Katrina had demolished several buildings and Keesler combined them into one huge new shopping complex and food court to serve the airmen and their families on the base and the many thousands of retired military who live in South Mississippi.

This was the first time I was back on the base since 1981 and I started having flashbacks when I saw the young airmen.

Paula and I spent an hour going over her plan for a sculpture inside the entrance of the building.

"I'm going to do a sculpture for you," I told her after touring the complex inside and out, "but I'm going to do it ten times bigger than you're asking for and I'm going to do it for free."

To do that where there was no tree, of course, meant planting a dead tree in concrete on the lawn front of the building. Bill Holmes, the executive director of the nearby Mississippi Coast Coliseum and Convention Center, had a tree that was nearly blown over by Katrina. His crews pulled it back upright, but Katrina won and the tree couldn't be saved.

The story continues...

It would live on at the Air Force base.

Keesler sent crews and equipment to get the tree. I came over from Florida and an engineer was there to make sure the huge oak didn't fall on the multi-million dollar parking garage under construction.

"I'll miss it by eight feet," I told him, using my trusty hand measurement to calculate where the tree would land. It fell just about perfectly – 10 feet from the garage.

"We lost a lot of magnificent trees during Hurricane Katrina. Marlin Miller, using his vision and extraordinary talent, took the remains of those trees and carved the many fish, birds, and mammals indigenous to the coast. Now we have magnificent works of art on display through-out the coastline to share with our neighbors and traveling guests."

- Bill Holmes

Executive Director, Mississippi Coast Coliseum and Convention Center

I marked the tree with large Xs to indicate exactly how it should face directly south when it was positioned in concrete at Keesler. Back in Florida, I got a call from the concrete crew asking about the positioning. Paula hurried over and called me back to say, "They got it." A 2005 penny, to mark the year of Hurricane Katrina, was planted with the tree in the concrete.

I came the next week and started carving the Air Force eagle with outspread wings.

The initial cuts took many hours.

The eagle finally taking shape.

General Dickinson thanking Marlin for his donation.

The finished eagle looking out towards the future.

Jerry Creel watches over the work

While I was sculpting the eagle outside the new BX and Commissary, a lot of retired military men and women who regularly spent time at the base came to watch.

But I was really surprised to see Jerry Creel there.

No matter where I was carving in Biloxi for more than a year, he would show up early in the morning in his Ford pickup. Sometimes he would stop and talk. Sometimes he'd just drive by.

That first day of carving at Keesler, nobody knew I was going to be there, not even Vincent Creel, Biloxi's public relations officer and Jerry Creel's son. Given the security check to get on the Air Force base, I was thinking as I got to work that day I wouldn't be seeing Mr. Creel today. I didn't know he was also retired from the military.

At 6:30 in the morning he drives by, making sure everything was right in Biloxi.

Dedication

The carving and the new building attracted the media from the Sun Herald newspaper, WLOX-TV and the local "Art Beat" television show hosted by Elaine Stevens from IP Casino Resort.

That was pretty crazy for a guy who came to Biloxi 30 years before as a trainee.

Brig. Gen. Ian Dickinson, the commander of Keesler Air Force Base, arrived only a few months before I started the eagle carving and we quickly connected.

He dedicated the eagle at the opening of the BX and Commissary, when 5,000 people came out to be a part of the celebration and to be the first to shop.

Archie Manning, the star New Orleans Saints quarterback and father of Peyton and Eli Manning, was there along with Congressman Gene Taylor and other elected officials and guests. Mark Michael made them spiral cut pens from the tree to mark the day.

A few months later I was invited to the retirement party for Keesler's Vice Commander, Col. Chris Valle. The event was at the Locker House, the building where I lived for nine months while I trained at Keesler. We had the premier dining facility at Keesler and people would come from across the base for breakfast. Being back there and having the eagle I carved soar at the new commissary completed my full-circle Keesler experience.

About Keesler Air Force Base

Known as "The Schoolhouse of the Air Force," Keesler Air Force Base is home to the Second Air Force and 81st Training Wing and is where many airmen go after basic training to learn meteorology, air traffic control and many other skills. In 2010, the base began training cyber warriors to fight in cyberspace.

Keesler also is home to the "Flying Jennies," who risk their lives in Iraq, Afghanistan and around the world, flying supplies and troops.

The Hurricane Hunters of the U.S. Air Force Reserve are based here. They flew through the eye of Hurricane Katrina, watched it head for the base and warned residents along the Coast to evacuate. Several of the Hurricane Hunters lost their homes to Katrina.

With nearly $1 billion in damage from the storm, the Air Force committed to rebuilding the base and launched Operation Dragon Comeback. More than 1,000 new homes were built to LEED environmentally friendly standards in the largest military and LEED residential building projects in the country's history.

The new base housing along with new dormitories, the rebuilt commissary and the new Bay Breeze Events Center on the golf course, overlooking the rebuilt marina, make Keesler one of the most coveted assignments in the Air Force.

The dedication plaque on Keesler's eagle wood sculpture.

Marlin presenting General Dickinson with a picture of the Col. Robert's eagle. It is on display in the new Robert's building on KAFB.

"I was always impressed with Marlin's ability to 'release' a beautiful creature from the remains of the storm-damaged trees on the Mississippi Gulf Coast. He has done so much to renew and beautify the coast and allow residents and visitors alike a new way to see beauty in the aftermath of such a terrible storm. Marlin was also a great friend to Keesler Air Force Base and it was always a true pleasure to have him add the beauty of his work to our base environment, like the incredible eagle statue dedicated in the front our new base shopping complex."

- General Ian R. Dickinson Commander, 81st Training Wing, Keesler Air Force Base, Mississippi

Lazarex Cancer Foundation

The first time I went beyond the Gulf Coast to carve a tree sculpture was in honor of my brother, Mike, from Wallace, North Carolina.

The Lazarex Cancer Foundation was having a "Hogs 'n Hens for Hope" fundraiser in North Carolina and I wanted to participate.

Mike died of pancreatic cancer in 2004. His wife, Erin, now heads the North Carolina chapter of the Lazarex Foundation. Their family story was the inspiration for the creation of the Lazarex Foundation, which helps defray the costs for end stage cancer patients to participate in FDA-approved clinical trials after they have exhausted all other options for treatment.

I brought a 700-pound cedar log with me from Florida to carve through the day into a 6-foot tall American eagle.

Dana Dornsife, President of Lazarex Cancer Foundation, with the 6' tall eagle.

Marlin carving the eagle for the live auction.

Pictures of the Katrina sculptures were displayed all around me while I worked and many people said they had seen the Katrina carvings on the NBC Nightly News.

When it came time to sell the carvings, the auctioneer upped the emotional appeal by telling the crowd about the Katrina sculptures and the resilience of South Mississippi.

That incited a bidding war and the eagle and seahorse sculptures ended up raising over $15,000.

Adding to that, Mark Michael came to the fundraiser from Naples, Florida, with two ballpoint pens he crafted from wood scraps of the Katrina trees. They were auctioned and raised another $380 and $395.

I find it amazing the Mississippi sculptures make such an impact, even far from the Coast where they stand.

Marlin on stage as the auctioneer tells the Katrina Sculpture story.

Lawrence Parks and Wendy Murphy Crumpler with the seahorse sculpture.

Dana Dornsife, a young guest, Erin Miller - Van Gorder , Wendy Murphy Crumpler and Marlin posing with the eagle.

Biloxi Town Green

After carving nearly two dozen sculptures in Biloxi and along the coast nearly every weekend for a year, I thought my mission in the city was complete.

Up and down the beach, dolphins frolicked in trees and wooden turtles, a seahorse and all sorts of marine animals became part of the new Coast scenery.

One place that didn't have any carvings was the Biloxi Town Green, an open park since Hurricane Katrina, along Highway 90 and just down from City Hall. Katrina washed away the historic house on the Green that served as the visitor center and the shoofly decks that encircled the oak trees in the park.

Any trees still standing were given care by crews of volunteers who treated the roots to counter the saltwater damage. Just when it seemed these trees that had stood for hundreds of years would survive, one lost its leaves and the arborist confirmed it had died.

That's when I started hearing from people around the city asking that I do one more Katrina sculpture for Biloxi.

A giant crane was used to prepare this tree for a sculpture.

At 25' tall, a single chainsaw cut can take hours to complete.

Marlin practically lived in the basket of this man lift for days in order to complete this giant sculpture.

Hundreds of tourists stopped by to take pictures of the aerial performance of sculptor Marlin Miller.

This was a big, fat tree and probably had the most historic significance of any tree I carved. The Town Green is where the annual Biloxi Seafood Festival and many other celebrations and services have been held for years. The cast and crew of ABC's Extreme Makeover Home Edition chose the Town Green as the site of the Katrina Memorial they built for the Mississippi Gulf Coast. It stands as high as the storm surge reached that day and is etched with the names of all who died in Mississippi during the storm.

I was in town when the huge tree was topped to prepare it for carving and watched a crane carefully lower each branch to the ground. Most of the wood was saved for commemorative pens and future carvings.

Biloxi Mayor A.J. Holloway always suggested I keep the carvings simple because most of them are viewed from a vehicle going 45 miles per hour down the highway. This carving was different. It was in a place where it would be part of the celebrations and the displays.

Still I angled the sculpture to the corner of the park where the arched entrance sign for the Biloxi Town Green frames the carving for those driving by. At the bottom a turtle climbs the tree and above the crab and mahi fish is a 17-foot marlin jumping toward the sky.

This was to be my grand finale for Biloxi and I thought what better time to complete it than when Biloxi was hosting the National Governors Conference in mid-July 2009. The governors were staying at the Beau Rivage Casino Resort close to the Town Green.

"Marlin has been blessed with a tremendous talent, and he used that gift to create breathtaking beauty along the Mississippi Gulf Coast. He sculpted beauty out of devastation. His work symbolizes rebirth and renewal. That message has spread across the nation from the exposure his work has received.

As a reporter, it was amazing to see him in action. Even more impressive was the fact that he wanted nothing back. He simply came to donate his time, energy and love to the Mississippi Gulf Coast to keep our story on the national/international radar. Marlin, his wife Rene, who also contributed her talents, and his children did more for the Gulf Coast than we could ever repay."

- Krystal Allan, Weekend Anchor/Reporter, WLOX - TV 13 - Biloxi, Ms.

Little did I know a political rally was booked the same weekend at the Town Green and the political tension kept away any governors, their staff and the usual on-lookers. The tree had issues, too. A hole in the oak had been filled with cement and long-forgotten square nails and electric insulators were hidden beneath the bark. They just knocked out chainsaw blades left and right as I worked.

July in Mississippi is always a challenge and it was so hot I worked 15 minutes on and 15 minutes off. Whether drawn to the Town Green by the political demonstrators or the carving in progress, news crews from Reuters and the Wall Street Journal who were in town to report on the Governors Conference came by and filmed and photographed as I carved.

RENE'S COLOR

Since it is in the center of Downtown Biloxi, we decided this sculpture needed some extra pop so Rene added her magic with color.

My wife was already well-experienced painting fish. I had carved about 200 life size Florida fish for the new Back Porch Restaurant in Panama City Beach, Florida. Because the walls were natural wood, the owners wanted colorful fish and Rene painted them all.

The restaurant is high profile, situated at the Pier Park shopping complex between Jimmy Buffett's Margaritaville and Guy Harvey's Island Grill, and so many colorful fish make it unforgettable.

Rene adding the final touches to her masterpiece.

At the Town Green, we were just going to use a dab of blue on two of the mahi fish. It looked so good Rene went on and added color to the blue crab, the green sea turtle and the vivid blue marlin, with cans of spray paint and a very sore trigger finger.

Some people were unhappy to see the natural color of the wood covered while others were excited to see the realistic sea life emerge with paint.

Even cute little puppies, like Saylor, get close to the tree sculptures...imagine that.

A few times while I worked the Biloxi Tour Train rolled into the Town Green. I heard the tour guide announce to the passengers, "He's here!" and they climbed out and listened to my stories about the Katrina sculptures.

Forty or so people were on board the day Rene painted, and they crowded around her, so delighted to be witnessing the carving getting its color.

" *That's just great. Thanks for doing that.*"

- Haley Barbour

Governor of Mississippi

The Dedication and Beyond

On Aug. 29, 2009, the memorial service for the 4th anniversary of Hurricane Katrina was held on the Town Green, as it was every other anniversary before and since.

Mayor A.J. Holloway and I rode a man lift to the top of the 24-foot tall sculpture and pulled off the cover to officially unveil the Katrina sculpture on the Green.

During the service four students recited the names of those who died during Hurricane Katrina. One of those students was Kendall Holloway, the mayor's niece and a senior at Biloxi High School.

I later heard from Kendall that her graduating class wanted to present a gift to the school and she asked me to do a carving. I turned a slab of the oak from the Town Green tree into an arrowhead plaque for the Biloxi Indians, tying together the students who stood strong after Katrina with the tree that had shaded generations on the Biloxi Town Green.

Marlin and Mayor Holloway unveiling Marlin's marlin.

Mississippi Emergency Management Agency Director Mike Womack presenting Marlin with a signed proclamation from Gov. Barbour declaring August 29, 2009 as Marlin Miller Day in the state of Mississippi.

Biloxi Public Affairs Manager Vincent Creel with his wife Natalie and sculptor Marlin Miller.

The Katrina Memorial built by the cast and crew of ABC's Extreme Makeover. It stands as high as the storm surge the day Katrina came to shore.

Vincent Creel shaking hands with the sculptor...sort of.

Mark Potter is a senior news correspondent for the NBC Nightly News with Brian Williams and MSNBC. He was on the Mississippi Gulf Coast for the 5th Anniversary of Katrina ceremonies. He provided great news stories during Katrina and again with the oil spill disaster.

Mark Potter of the NBC News network checks out the enlarged picture of the American Profile magazine cover and article about Marlin Miller and the Katrina Sculptures. On August 29, 2010, the American Profile magazine featured this story and printed over 10 million copies for nearly 20 million readers across the country. This weekend tabloid reminded the rest of the country that the Gulf Coast has had to endure both natural and manmade disasters in recent years, but continues to stay strong and resilient.

U.S. Congressman Gene Taylor talking to Sculptor Marlin Miller during the 5th Anniversary of Katrina ceremony at the Town Green in Biloxi. He also signed one of Marlin's sculptures to be used for a future fundraiser.

U.S. Senator Roger Wicker talking with sculptor Marlin Miller. He was also kind enough to sign the oak sculpture for a fundraiser.

Keesler AFB Commander General Andrew Mueller talking to Marlin before the ceremony. At right is former Biloxi Mayor Danny Guice.

General Kory Cornum, Keesler AFB, talking to Marlin after the ceremony.

PUBLIC ART EXHIBITS

The Katrina sculptures have become ambassadors to the Coast. When people hear about the carvings on television and read about them in newspapers and magazines, they want to come to South Mississippi and see them in person.

After Hurricane Katrina and again after the Gulf oil disaster, millions were spent on advertising campaigns to bring people back to the hotels, casinos, restaurants and the beach. The carvings continue to do that for free and they've become the number one tourist attraction on the Mississippi Gulf Coast.

Gulfport-Biloxi International Airport

At the Gulfport-Biloxi International Airport, officials set up an art program and installed a 52-foot glass display where passengers can admire the art while they wait for takeoff. Airport director Bruce Frallic and Jeremiah Gerald, the airport's director of air service and business development, asked if I could fill half of the case with carvings and then asked if I could fill the whole display. Instead of a few months, they wanted to keep the carvings on display for a year, changing them every few months to keep the display fresh.

This deer head is one of several sculptures at the airport exhibit . It is created from many pieces of driftwood delivered to the Mississippi beaches by Hurricane Katrina.

In 52 feet, passengers see sculptures, photographs of the Katrina carvings along Beach Boulevard, presentations I received from Gov. Haley Barbour and the recent award from the Phenomenal People event on the 5th anniversary of Hurricane Katrina. Looping on a flat screen television are the NBC Nightly News feature with Mark Potter and the PBS documentary with Walt Grayson.

This is an especially important project for me. So many people fly in to visit the casinos, but they never touch the soul of South Mississippi. The airport setting makes them a captive audience and allows them to take home an understanding of the Coast story.

I know it's had an impact because I've gotten e-mails from Connecticut, New Hampshire and all over the northern part of the country from people who saw the airport display and felt enough connection to take the time to write.

U.S. Rep. Gene Taylor said he checks the display every time he flies out of Gulfport. Mark Potter called me after landing at the airport and seeing the display. He flew directly to the Coast from Mexico, where he was riding with the president and reporting from the worst area of the drug wars.

"I'm standing here at the airport looking at you," Potter said over the phone. I told him to check out the television and he'd see himself in the display.

As an artist it's exciting to touch people with the Katrina sculptures and to draw a lot of attention to the beautiful beach in Biloxi and South Mississippi.

The "Wild Mustang" is one of the featured sculptures in the exhibit. It was made from over 200 pieces of driftwood found on the Mississippi shores after Hurricane Gustav.

This driftwood sea turtle received special attention after the Gulf oil spill. Over 1,000 turtles have been recovered since the oil crisis.

"Marlin's display at the Gulfport– Biloxi International Airport is a symbol of the spirit of optimism, renewal and hope that is the essence of the people of the Mississippi Gulf Coast. Passengers can't help but to stop and examine the intricate details and natural beauty of each piece. For visitors, the display serves as a welcome, a first impression of their destination. For locals, it's a reminder that helps renew and strengthen those core values learned from challenges of the past."

- Jeremiah Gerald, CM

Director of Air Services and Business Development

Gulfport - Biloxi International Airport

The new Gulfport-Biloxi International Airport is a beautiful facility that attracts thousands of visitors a day to the Gulf Coast.

Mississippi Welcome Center

The Jackson County Mississippi Welcome Center on Interstate 10 holds the Marlin Miller art display encouraging travelers to take a tour of the Highway 90 Coast.

Mississippi Welcome Center

When the Deepwater Horizon rig exploded and oil began pouring into the Gulf of Mexico, people on the Coast were most upset about the danger to the dolphins, pelicans and other sea life. The Katrina sculptures became a symbol of what the Gulf Coast stood to lose.

The oil disaster also drove visitors away from the Coast in the peak tourist season. Normally during the summer the white sand beaches see families romping in the sand and flying kites and teams playing sand volleyball. The summer of 2010, the only people on the beach were crews looking for oil.

I had the idea before the oil spill to set up a display of carvings at the Welcome Center on Interstate 10, where people entering Mississippi from Alabama are offered a cold beverage and a warm welcome.

The State agreed and Pauletta, who runs the Jackson County Welcome Center, helped make it happen.

NBC Nightly News with Brian Williams came to the Marlin Miller Studio to film the creation of the large eagle that now resides at the Mississippi Welcome Center. The eagle has been dedicated to Rene's cousin, Joshua Ragsdale, a Mississippi native and a Nashville singer/ songwriter, who passed away from cancer in July 2010.

Marlin's grandson, Keller, inspecting the large eagle prior to its delivery to the welcome center.

Pauletta Charlton, Supervisor of the Jackson County Welcome Center, assisting Marlin with the art exhibit.

The main parlor at the Welcome Center holds the art exhibit and the Katrina Sculpture information to help detour travelers to the coast.

Again I brought in a flat screen TV with a loop of the video from NBC Nightly News and the PBS story, along with some literature people could take with them. A 7-foot tall, 500-pound eagle is the centerpiece of the display that also has a tarpon fish, a seahorse, turtle and shark. We'll change out the sculptures from time to time and eventually get a map people can follow from the interstate down to the beach to see the carvings.

There's been incredible feedback, with visitors from Denmark, Canada, Belgium, South Africa and across America saying they thought they would make a detour off I-10 down to the beach to see the Katrina sculptures.

When I carve the eagle at the Infinity Science Center in Hancock County at the western boundary of Mississippi, the sculptures will welcome visitors arriving at both ends of the state and hopefully draw them to the beach, the restaurants and gift shops and to the people and hospitality of South Mississippi.

Hurricane Katrina.....The 5th Anniversary

With the 5th anniversary of Hurricane Katrina four months away it seemed the Mississippi Coast was making a steady recovery and tourists were returning to the beaches.

Then oil started pouring into the Gulf of Mexico from the Deepwater Horizon well and the fear was another major disaster was heading for the coast.

NBC Nightly News reporter Mark Potter called to see how the oil was impacting us and came to our Florida house to film another "Making a Difference" feature. We took him out in our boat and he used footage from the original story to put Mississippi's Katrina Sculptures back in the spotlight. The NBC Nightly News with Brian Williams has now produced three features on the Katrina Sculptures.

Governor Haley Barbour wanted to show the country the Mississippi coast was spared from much oil reaching the beaches. He was instrumental in getting the CW Network to film "The Gulf Is Back," featuring a concert at the Coast Coliseum and video from sites across the Mississippi Coast.

American Idol star Ace Young and I climbed up into a Katrina Sculpture for a different camera angle and he interviewed me for the music special.. After airing on CW, the show was picked up and seen on the Hallmark Channel.

NBC correspondent Mark Potter with Erica, the producer, looking out over the Gulf of Mexico with Rene and Marlin.

A succession of good things happened leading up to the Katrina anniversary. A pelican I carved was dedicated at the new Mississippi Coast Convention Center Pelican Café. There I was on the cover of American Profiles magazine, which was inserted in over 10 million newspapers around the country on the weekend of August 29, standing in front of the towering sculpture on the Biloxi Town Green.

That got the attention of public television in Iowa, where I grew up, and they plan to broadcast Walt Grayson's nine-minute Mississippi Roads documentary in Iowa.

The Katrina Sculptures are about complete, but I continue to use some of the cuttings from the tree to make sculptures for fundraising events on the coast. For a "Making Strides Against Breast Cancer" fundraiser at the Hard Rock Café , Biloxi, I saw a slab of wood from the oak in the Town Green in my workshop and carved it into a guitar. Then I carved an arm to hold it upright and asked celebrities performing on the coast to sign it to make this guitar rock.

Ace Young and Marlin Miller were really "up a tree" filming this segment of the music special.

Mayor Longo and Ace Young with Preston.

Rene with Ace

Those Katrina Sculptures in South Mississippi have really branched out. Gail Cunningham is talking about a sculpture for the national kickoff of the Great American Cleanup in Phoenix.

Lee County Commissioner Frank Mann heard about the Katrina Sculptures and he asked what I could do with a massive oak tree that's dropping branches outside the county courthouse in Fort Myers, Florida. There is a beautiful sculpture inside of that tree.

High above the ground, Marlin inspects the tree.

Several TV crews showed up to see if Marlin would agree to carve their massive oak. The tree is 28' around and full of old steel bolts.

The "crazy" sculptor with Commissioner Frank Mann in Fort Myers, Florida

A&E's Billy the Exterminator and Marlin kicked off the Phenomenal People events at the Treasure Bay Casino.

Rene, Ricky, Billy and Marlin.

Miss Mississippi Jr. Teen McKenzie Irish presenting Marlin with his Phenomenal People Award. Actor Morgan Freeman was in the audience.

Marlin and Rene were backstage guests of Jay Leno and the Gulf Coast Community Foundation at the Beau Rivage. Jay raised $100,000 for the event.

Thank you Mr. Leno!

Melissa Medley, Mississippi Marketing Director, and Governor Barbour talking with Marlin at the Convention Center Grand Opening.

Gail McGovern, President and CEO of the American Red Cross, speaking with Marlin about a fundraising event.

Marlin present the First Lady of Mississippi Marsha Barbour with an oak pen for all the work she did after Katrina.

Governor Barbour and Marlin at the Fallen Oak Country Club. Marlin's sculptures were used as trophies for the 2010 Governor's Cup. This tournament has raised millions for charity.

MSNBC and The Weather Channel gave live broadcasts out of Biloxi on August 29, 2010, the 5th anniversary of Hurricane Katrina.

NASA INFINITY

At the western entrance to Mississippi, just this side of the Louisiana line on Interstate 10, will be an amazing experience when Infinity Science Center opens.

A team of such dedicated individuals put more than a decade into conceiving, planning, funding, designing and now building Infinity adjacent to the Mississippi Welcome Center. Hurricane Katrina stepped in the way of their progress, and some who started the mission left this world before it will be completed.

Their dream was to engage visitors, especially students, and immerse them in the oceans, the land and the stars.

The goal is to create a science center and visitor attraction; "A place like no other, where curiosity is nurtured and discovery is rewarded."

How honored I am to be asked to play a small part in that experience.

A photograph of the billboard that sits at the future location of the Infinity Center.

John Wilson, Myron Webb and James Huk, who are among those working to bring Infinity to South Mississippi, asked if they could hire me to carve a sculpture at the entrance of Infinity. I told them I'd love to do it and donate the carving.

For inspiration they invited me along with my family to Kennedy Space Center in Florida to experience the final liftoff of the space shuttle Atlantis. Talk about inspiration.

Head of NASA, Charles Bolden and granddaughters speaking with Marlin and his family.

Preston with his dad at the launch site waiting for the final liftoff of space shuttle Atlantis.

We learned first-hand what it's like to be in space from Astronaut David Wolf, who has made four shuttle missions and a record seven space walks.

We toured Kennedy Space Center, met Charles Bolden, the head of NASA, and sat with the astronauts' families as Atlantis launched.

The astronauts and their missions, including Apollo 13 Astronaut Fred Haise, who grew up in Biloxi, Mississippi and is dedicated to Infinity, will be my inspiration when I carve a large eagle outside Infinity.

We've already located the huge tree that will be planted there. Metal from retired NASA projects will be incorporated into the mixed media sculpture. I envision neon lights through metal wings in keeping with the contemporary architecture of the science center.

The eagle may not be able to soar to space despite its NASA parts, but visitors young and old will reach the stars through the exhibits and experiences at Infinity Science Center.

Astronaut David Wolf explaining the re-entry process and extreme heat and vibration experienced when returning through the atmosphere.

John Wilson, Marlin Miller, My-ron Webb, and Jim Huk discussing the large sculpture project for the Infinity.

"It was a late fall day in 2009 at the harbor in Long Beach, MS that first brought our families together. As Rene, you and your family moved swiftly to put you art work away due to the ominous storm clouds moving in, Linda and I stood in awe and marveled at your artwork and the opportunity of a lifetime to meet the man and his family responsible for the Mississippi Gulf Coast Carvings that line Highway 90. As I said to you then, there are not many times I have driven down Highway 90 past one of your sculptures where there has not been someone from all walks of life taking a photograph next to your sculptures.

Your sculptures stand today, like the majestic live oaks once stood as a poignant reminder of the resiliency of humans to persevere through all the tragedy of Hurricane Katrina"

- Jim and Linda Huk

NASA Contracting Officer

Infinity Experience

Infinity Science Center is designed to make science exciting and fun.

Outdoors will be rockets and science activities. Inside, visitors who have time for just a quick stop will still be able to get a sample of the museum through Science Express, a free exhibit where they can map the ocean floor, test the strength of a building against hurricane force winds and design and launch a virtual rocket.

When they return for a day at Infinity, the 3-D Immersive Theater will fly them "from the depths of the ocean to the farthest reaches of space" and back to the Gulf Coast and Stennis Space Center, where every rocket engine that has ever launched Americans into space was tested.

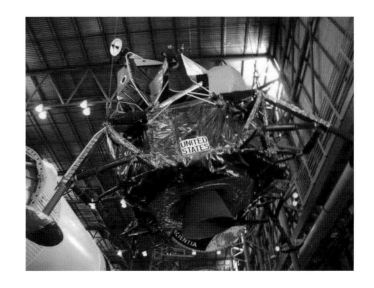

A lunar lander on exhibit at the Kennedy Space Center.

Preston and Samantha posing with a picture of the Atlantis crew.

Visitors will discover the wonders of the Earth Gallery and Space Gallery. Those who want to be fully immersed in the experience can become "scientists in training" on one of six guided missions.

The experience of Infinity Science Center was designed by Edwin Schlossberg's ESI Design, which has created the experiences for the Statue of Liberty-Ellis Island and many other renowned exhibits and museums.

Preston and his mom standing under an Apollo rocket.

Chocolate space shuttles at the reception dinner.

Sam and her dad standing with the astronauts listening to Mr. Bolden speak.

Preston and Sam in front of the "splash down" module.

"Marlin's carvings of hurricane damaged trees along the Mississippi gulf coast have raised the spirits of all who drive by from the dismal days following Katrina. I am particularly proud that Marlin plans to put one of his "out of this world" sculptures at the "out of this world" Infinity at Stennis Space Center!"

- Fred Haise

Apollo 13 Astronaut

JOURNEY OF MEMORIES

Special thanks to these beautiful casino resorts.
The partnership you built with Marlin contributed
to the success of this project.

Romy Simpson preparing Marlin for the "Good Morning Mississippi" show with Rhonda Weidner.

"The regal tree sculptures envisioned in Marlin's heart were patiently carved one by one and brought healing to South Mississippi serving as a tribute to the unyielding spirit of its people. When I drive down highway 90, I see his art carved in nature's remnants of Katrina devastation, and I am inspired by his epic gift! These tree sculptures were created selflessly.

They have become the cornerstones of the rebuilding efforts and have provided an extraordinary destination attraction for the young and old. Mr. Miller's work is a constant beacon of hope and he is a hero to the people!"

- Romy Simpson

Owner, Negrotto's Fine Art Gallery

Paula Strawn, Keesler AFB Exchange, talking to Marlin inside the new $60 million shopping complex.

Mary Perez, Sun Herald newspaper, visiting with Rene and Marlin.

Mark Potter giving Marlin a tour of the satellite truck.

Marlin taking a break in Long Beach.

Coastal residents have made it a tradition to decorate the sculptures for Christmas and Mardi Gras.

The beautiful Biloxi Harbor.

Biloxi paid a contractor seven thousand dollars for these garden carvings, prior to Marlin's involvement.

"Seagull Rest Stop"

Pass Christian Harbor

The owls eyes have become a popular "collector's item."

Marlin's sculptures come in all shapes and sizes.

Dolphins in the sky.

Marlin with his "Door for Ohr" and "Woody", the convention center's restaurant mascot.

Marlin sporting sunglasses made by Suzanne Johnson's daughter Piper.

Marlin's wife Rene and her sister, Teresa, enjoying "The Gulf is Back" concerts.

Rene and Teresa with Lone Star.

Rene, David Hasselhoff and Teresa.

Marlin with Bo Bice at "The Gulf is Back" concert taping.

Taylor Hicks entertaining the crowd.

Marlin with his wife Rene and in-laws Michael and Teresa.

Marlin in his work environment.

Biloxi five year status

In the days and weeks after Hurricane Katrina, the question was raised over and over by those surveying the damage. "How long do you think it will take to recover?" Initially, in those long and sweltering days immediately after Katrina, "five to seven years" seemed like a safe and sufficient time frame.

In time, as the issues of rebuilding came to light, a more analytical response surfaced: "Some areas of our city will rebuild quickly. Some will take longer than others and some, for better and worse, will never return to the way they were, given the challenges of the cost and availability of insurance and the expense of new construction requirements."

Katrina claimed 5,000 homes and businesses in Biloxi, about a quarter of the housing stock in the city, primarily in east Biloxi and in areas along the waterfront. Tens of thousands of construction permits have been issued since the storm, primarily for repairs to existing homes and businesses. The fact is, less than 800 building permits have been issued for single family homes. Hundreds of thousands of volunteers, in a humanitarian effort the size of which has never been seen in the history of this country, have helped rehabilitate thousands of homes in Biloxi and the surrounding area.

Today, at the five-year point, the Biloxi recovery remains a study in contrasts. Some areas of the city – the casino resort sector and those residential and commercial areas away from the water – have indeed rebuilt, providing thousands of jobs and an engine to drive Biloxi's storied hospitality industry. Other areas – Point Cadet and other waterfront areas vulnerable to storm waters – are still defining their future.

The very characteristics that have made Biloxi such an inviting locale over the years -- a city on a peninsula with two rivers running through it, countless bayous and streams, and bounded by a bay and a gulf -- are making the recovery such a daunting challenge. The national recession, which tied up access to venture capital and retarded economic growth, only exacerbated the situation.

Virtually every public facility in Biloxi sustained some level of damage or was destroyed. No building, no person was untouched by this storm. However, the city, has made significant progress on restoring or rebuilding its municipal facilities. Of the three dozen major projects – ranging from restoration of the city's surviving historic properties, City Hall, marinas and harbors, historic properties, and ball fields and parks – a third have been completed, a third are under construction and a third are nearing construction.

A separate phase of the city's rebuilding effort -- a $355 million project that will see the repair or replacement or virtually every street, sidewalk, curb and gutter that went underwater -- appears to have navigated the changing currents of the federal bureaucracy and is ready to begin construction. The project will see as much as 25 years worth of major infrastructure work compressed into a five to seven year time frame. Never will Biloxi have witnessed such a massive public enterprise.

Longtime residents in Biloxi realize that rebuilding from unprecedented storms – whether Camille or Katrina – does not occur overnight, particularly when done in a responsible manner, one that will reduce the threat from future storms. While Biloxi's rebuilding remains a study in contrasts, Biloxi's will remains a constant. The city will be rebuilt, it will recover, and it will emerge a better city and a better people.

Get a detailed look at Biloxi's recovery online at biloxi.ms.us

- Vincent Creel

Conclusion

Any day you drive Highway 90 you'll see people snapping photographs of the Katrina Sculptures. Crews in Biloxi and other coast cities spray the carvings with a sealant to keep out the salt spray, bugs and UV rays so the eagles and dolphins will be around for many years.

The carvings got more adventurous as the trees I carved got bigger and people became harder to impress. I'm determined to make the eagle at Infinity Science Center something spectacular.

I've heard from an artist in Galveston, Texas, who said he carved some trees there that were damaged by Hurricane Ike. He said he was inspired by my work. Seeing the impact the Katrina Sculptures had on the Mississippi Coast, I would like to reach out to people across the country after tornados, floods, ice storms and other disasters and turn their broken trees and lives into art. I hope they will find in it the same symbol of resilience inspired by the people of the Mississippi coast.

I'm doing the work for free as a heartfelt gift that is more valuable because there isn't a price tag attached.

When you give something away it comes back to you. I hope what I've done inspires other artists. I especially hope it inspired my kids, who saw how one person can make a difference – even Dad.

marlinmm61@aol.com

Marlinmillergallery.com